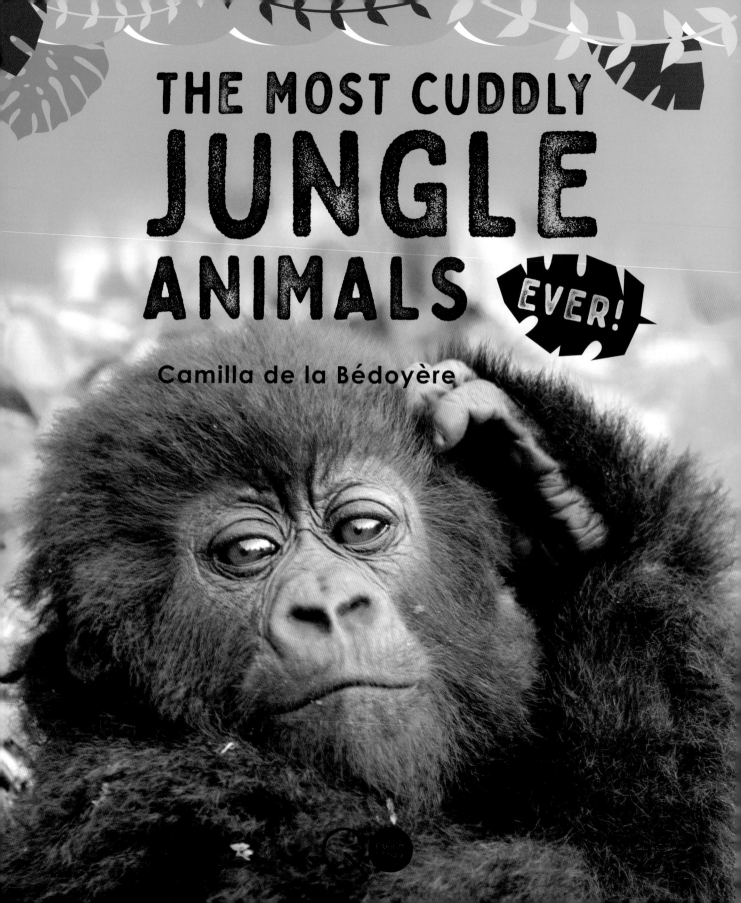

THE MOST CUDDLY JUNGLE ANIMALS EVER!

Camilla de la Bédoyère

Author: Camilla de la Bédoyère
Editor: Emily Pither
Designer: Cloud King Creative
Picture Researcher: Sarah Bell

This library edition published by Quarto Library,
an imprint of The Quarto Group.
26391 Crown Valley Parkway, Suite 220
Mission Viejo, CA 92691, USA
T: +1 949 380 7510
F: +1 949 380 7575
www.QuartoKnows.com

Distributed in the United States and Canada by
Lerner Publisher Services
241 First Avenue North
Minneapolis, MN 55401 U.S.A.
www.lernerbooks.com

A CIP record for this book is available from the
Library of Congress.

ISBN 978-0-7112-7224-8

Manufactured in Guangdong, China TT082021

9 8 7 6 5 4 3 2 1

The Jungle Stats contain
information about the
color, size, cuddliness
rating, and location of
each animal.

JUNGLE STATS

Color: Black

Size: 4 to 6 feet tall

Central and
western Africa

CONTENTS

BUSHBABY

Bushbabies spend the hot day fast asleep in jungle trees.

At sunset, a bushbaby stirs from its rest and sets off to hunt. It can twist and turn its large ears to listen for bugs, lizards, and birds. It catches them with its tiny hands.

JUNGLE STATS

Color: Brown to gray

Size: Up to 16 inches long

African jungles

5

CLOUDED LEOPARD

The clouded leopard is one of the most beautiful cats in the world. The blotches on its soft fur look like clouds.

Few people have been lucky enough to see a clouded leopard because these fluffy hunters are very shy and they spend most of their time hiding in trees.

JUNGLE STATS

Color: Cream and reddish fur with black marks

Size: Up to 3.5 feet long

Southeast Asia

SLOTH

It's hard to see a sleepy sloth in a tree. Its furry coat has tiny plants living in it, so it looks green, just like the leaves high in the treetops.

Sloths have long, curved claws that they use to hang upside-down.

JUNGLE STATS

Color: Dark brown, red-brown, gray

Size: 18 to 35 inches long

Central and South America

GIBBON

Gibbons are the kings of the swingers! They have very long arms and they use them to hang from trees and swing from branch to branch.

A baby uses its little hands to cling tightly to its mom's fur as she races through the trees.

JUNGLE STATS

Color: Cream, gray, black, or brown

Size: Up to 3 feet tall

Jungles of Southeast Asia

RUFOUS BETTONG

This cuddly little animal hops like a mini-kangaroo!

It has a long, bendy tail that it uses to grab bunches of grass. It uses the grass to make a nest on the dry forest floor, where it sleeps in the day. Rufous bettongs keep their babies in a pouch.

JUNGLE STATS

Color: Red-brown and gray

Size: Up to 21 inches long

Forests of Australia

GORILLA

These big, hairy apes live in family groups. The father gorilla looks after his family.

Baby gorillas love to play in the jungle. When they are tired, they sneak back to mom for a kiss and a cuddle.

JUNGLE STATS

Color: Black

Size: 4 to 6 feet tall

Central and western Africa

DHOLE

Dholes are shy, wild dogs that live in Asia. They have red-brown fur and long, bushy tails that they wag, just like pet dogs.

Baby dholes are called pups and they are gray-brown. Dholes are playful animals and they love to jump around in water on a hot day.

JUNGLE STATS

Color: Reddish-brown with cream parts

Size: Up to 18 inches long

Southeast Asia

JAGUAR

The jaguar is a water-loving jungle cat. It has a strong body and can climb, leap, run, and swim.

It uses its long tail to help it balance when it walks along branches. The spotty marks on a jaguar's fur are called rosettes.

JUNGLE STATS

Color: Fawn, cream, and black

Size: Up to 6 feet long

Central and South America

TARSIER

A tarsier may be small, but it's a fast and nimble hunter.

It has big eyes and a long tail with a cute tuft of fur on the tip. Tarsiers hold tight onto a tree and then leap. They jump between trees to grab insects, bats, and birds.

JUNGLE STATS

Color: Reddish-brown

Size: 4 to 6 inches long

Southeast Asia

INDIAN GIANT SQUIRREL

These colorful squirrels with big, bushy tails are at home in the treetops. They can leap more than 16.4 feet between branches.

Squirrels build nests from leaves and twigs and keep their babies safe there while they grow bigger.

JUNGLE STATS

Color: Dark red to brown with cream patches

Size: 14 to 16 inches long

Forests of India

BLACK AND WHITE RUFFED LEMUR

Lovely lemurs are monkey-like animals with thick fur and a long tail.

Lemurs climb through the trees, carefully picking fruit off the branches. Some lemurs carry their babies with them, but others leave the youngsters in a nest. Ruffed lemurs make loud barking sounds when they see danger.

JUNGLE STATS

Color: Black and white

Size: Up to 4 feet long

Island of Madagascar, near Africa

ORANGUTAN

Orangutans are big apes that live in the rainforests of Asia.

They love to climb trees and eat the juicy fruits that grow in the forest. Their favorite is the durian fruit, which smells like stinky socks!

JUNGLE STATS

Color: Red-orange

Size: Up to 4.5 feet tall

Borneo and Sumatra in Southeast Asia

COTTON-TOP TAMARIN

The fluffy white fur on a tamarin's head is called a crest or crown.

Cotton-top tamarins live together in big families and they take care of each other. They even use their claws to brush each other's fur to keep it clean and shiny!

JUNGLE STATS

Color: Black and white

Size: 8 to 10 inches long

Colombia, South America

SLOTH BEAR

A sloth bear's thick fur coat is black and shaggy.

These bears walk slowly through the forest, digging up termite nests and sucking up the little bugs. Sloth bears climb trees and hang upside down from the branches!

JUNGLE STATS

Color: Black

Size: 4 to 6 feet long

Southeast Asia

PHOTO CREDITS